Celebrations

Divali

Denise Jordan

www.raintreepublishers.co.uk
Visit our website to find out more information about Raintree books.

To order:
☎ Phone 44 (0) 1865 888112
🖹 Send a fax to 44 (0) 1865 314091
💻 Visit the Raintree Bookshop at www.raintreepublishers.co.uk to browse catalogue and order online.

First published in Great Britain by Raintree, Halley Court, Jordan Hill, Oxford OX2 8EJ, part of Harcourt Education.
Raintree is a registered trademark of Harcourt Education Ltd.

© Harcourt Education Ltd 2003
First published in paperback in 2004
The moral right of the proprietor has been asserted.

Editorial: Jennifer Gillis (HL-US) and Diyan Leake
Design: Sue Emerson (HL-US) and Michelle Lisseter
Picture Research: Amor Montes de Oca (HL-US) and Maria Joannou
Production: Lorraine Hicks

Originated by Dot Gradations
Printed and bound in China by South China Printing Company

10 digit ISBN 1 844 21521 0 (hardback)
13 digit ISBN 978 1 844 21521 8 (hardback)
07 06 05 04
10 9 8 7 6 5 4 3 2
10 digit ISBN 1 844 21526 1 (paperback)
13 digit ISBN 978 1 844 21526 3 (paperback)
12 11 10 09
10 9 8 7 6

British Library Cataloguing in Publication Data
Jordan, Denise
Divali
394.2'6545
A full catalogue record for this book is available from the British Library.

Acknowledgements
The publishers would like to thank the following for permission to reproduce photographs: Corbis pp. **5** (Arvind Garg), **6** (AFP), **8** (Joseph Sohm/ChromoSohm Inc.), **17** (Catherine Karnow), **18** (Earl & Nazima Kowall), **23** (Hindu, Arvind Garg; kurta, Catherine Karnow; sparkler, Earl & Nazima Kowall), back cover (sparkler, Earl & Nazima Kowall); Dinodia Photo Library pp. **4** (Omni-Photo Communications), **7** (D. Banerjeb), **10** (D. Banerjeb), **13** (Omni-Photo Communications), **19** (Ranjit Sen), **23** (diva, D. Banerjeb); rangoli, Omni-Photo Communications); Drik/Abir Abdullah pp. **21**, **22**, **24**; PhotoEdit, Inc./Rudi Von Briel pp. **16**, **23** (sari), **24**; Robert Lifson p. **15**; Stock Transparency Services Images pp. **9**, **11**; TRIP/H. Rogers pp. **12**, **14**, **20**, **23** (toran), back cover (toran)

Cover photograph reproduced with permission of Dinodia Photo Library (Omni-Photo Communications)

Every effort has been made to contact copyright holders of any material reproduced in this book. Any omissions will be rectified in subsequent printings if notice is given to the publishers.

Some words are shown in bold, **like this.** You can find them in the glossary on page 23.

Contents

What is Divali? 4

When do people celebrate Divali? 6

What do people do during Divali? 8

What lights are there during Divali? . . 10

What do Divali decorations look like?. . 12

What food do people eat
    during Divali?. 14

How do people dress for Divali? 16

What do children do during Divali? . . 18

Do people give presents for Divali?. . . 20

Quiz. 22

Glossary 23

Index 24

Answers to quiz 24

What is Divali?

Divali is a special time.

It is a celebration for **Hindu** people all over the world.

On Divali, Hindu people celebrate
the new year.

When do people celebrate Divali?

People celebrate Divali in the autumn.

It is in October or November.

People might celebrate Divali for
more than one day.

What do people do during Divali?

People clean their houses to get ready for Divali.

They have fairs and dance in the streets.

Family and friends get together.

They share food and tell stories.

What lights are there during Divali?

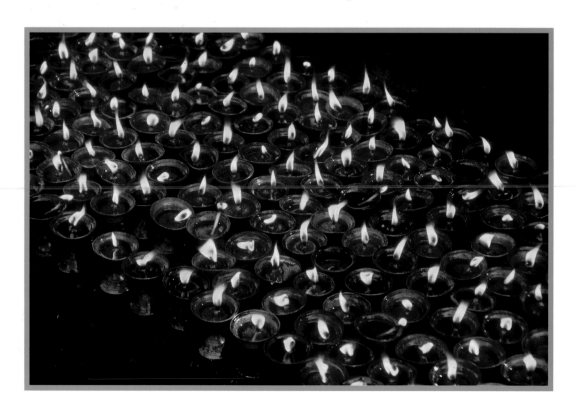

Divali means 'row of lights'.

People have oil lamps called **divas** in their homes.

People put strings of lights around their houses.

Fireworks light up the night.

What do Divali decorations look like?

Many people place a **toran** over their front door.

A toran is made from flowers or cloth.

In some places, women and children draw on the floor.

The drawings are called **rangoli**.

What food do people eat during Divali?

Milk is a special food for **Hindu** people.

During Divali, people eat sweets made from milk.

| barfi | ladoo | cham cham |

Children eat sweets called barfi, ladoos and cham chams.

How do people dress for Divali?

sari

Women and girls wear new **saris**.

A sari is a cloth wrapped around the body.

kurta

Men and boys wear new **kurtas**.

A kurta is a long, loose shirt.

What do children do during Divali?

Some children light sparklers.

Children may also put on plays.

Do people give presents for Divali?

People may send each other Divali cards.

Divali is a special time for giving.

Quiz

Here are some things you see during Divali.

Can you name them?

Look for the answers on page 24.

?   ?

Glossary

diva
special oil lamp

Hindu
person who follows the main religion
in India

kurta
long, loose Indian shirt

rangoli
special patterns people make using
coloured powder

sari
long cloth that Indian girls and women wrap
around the body and over the shoulder

toran
a decoration hung over a door

Index

barfi 15

cards 20

cham chams 15

decorations 12

divas 10, 23

fireworks 11

food 9, 14

Hindu 4, 5, 14, 23

kurtas 17, 23

ladoos 15

lights 10, 11

milk 14

plays 19

rangoli 13, 23

saris 16, 23

sparklers 18

stories 9

sweets 14, 15

toran 12, 23

Answers to quiz on page 22

diva   sari